t'

With gratitude.

Jenifer Lanrognt

The ABCs of the S.Y.V.

Charleston, SC
www.PalmettoPublishing.com

The ABCs of the S.Y.V.
Copyright © 2021 by Jenifer Sanregret

First Edition

Hardcover ISBN: 978-1-63837-881-5
Paperback ISBN: 978-1-63837-877-8

The ABCs of the S.Y.V.

An Alphabetical Journey Through the Santa Ynez Valley

Jenifer Sanregret

illustrated by Karla Dueñas

Dedicated to Vance and Hayes, page 7 is for us.
To my husband, thank you for the endless support in everything I do.

Special thanks to everyone who has taken the time to teach me something about the S.Y. Valley.

This is for you!

A is for Aebleskiver, a popular Danish treat.
They are freshly made and ready to eat.
You can share with friends or fill your belly.
Whatever you choose, don't forget the jelly!

B is for Ballard, the smallest of the towns.
Back in 1883, it had the only schoolhouse around.
Until the 1950s, the Little Red Schoolhouse had no electricity.
It's true! It was a time of sweet simplicity.

C is for Carriage- the transportation in the olden days.
The Santa Ynez Museum has one that still sways.
With four wheels they are pulled by a horse or two.
And they sit up high, so you have a good view.

D is for Deodar Cedar, the trees lined up in Buellton.
It is such a sight to see while driving through them.
There are a hundred trees that soar over seventy feet.
If you were to climb one, the view couldn't be beat!

E is for Equestrian, it means "horseback riding".
Here the horses on hillsides seem to be gliding.
From barrel racing, vaulting, and roping,
You'll see all types of riders out loping.

6

F is for Farmers Market- that is set up, rain or shine.
Buy local vegetables, and fruit, like grapes on a vine.
The options change depending on the weather.
It's hard work, so always say, "Thank you, farmers!"

7

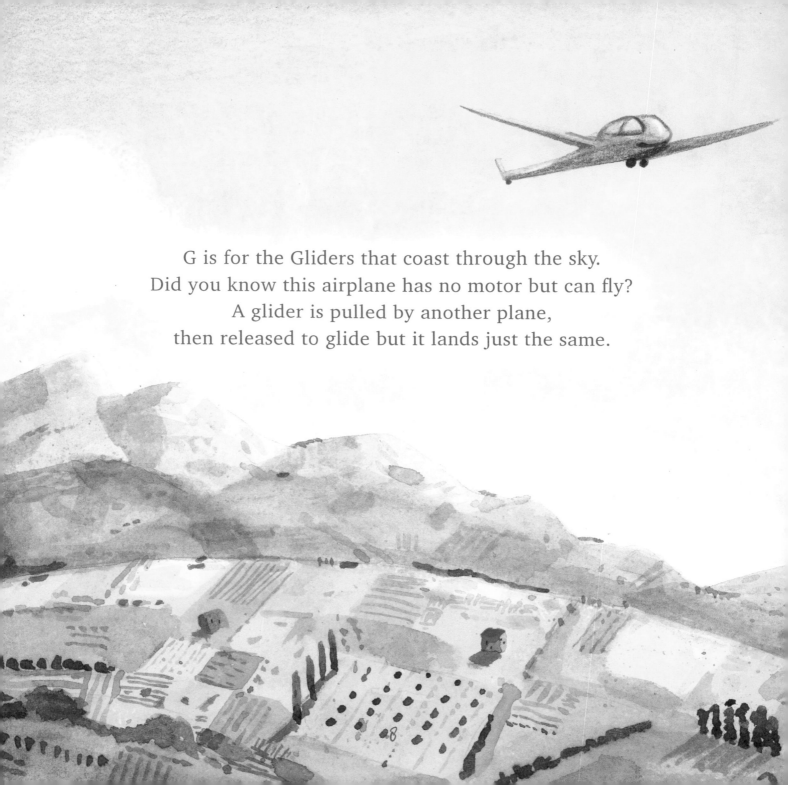

G is for the Gliders that coast through the sky.
Did you know this airplane has no motor but can fly?
A glider is pulled by another plane,
then released to glide but it lands just the same.

H is for Hot air balloon, another motorless aircraft.
In 1783, the first passengers went up and it was a laugh!
Because the first was a pig, the second was a sheep,
and the last was a rooster, who didn't make a peep.

I is for Ice Cream, Solvang's best treat!
You'll need it to beat the summer heat.
Any flavor will do when it's almost 100 degrees.
Grab a cone or a sundae and eat all you please.

J is for Jule Fest, our festive winter holiday.
A month-long celebration of cheer on display.
This tradition includes a "Nisse", the Christmas gnome.
A happy-looking man who is said to protect your home.

K is for Klomp, the wooden Dutch shoe.
Klomp stands for one and klompen means two.
The Danish call them clogs, yet they are just alike,
using wood leaving the inside hollow
to fit your foot just right.

L is for Los Olivos—Spanish for "the olives" is what it means.
This sweet town dates all the way back to the 1860s.
Known for the flagpole right in the center,
which is also the Christmas tree that's lit in December.

13

M is for the Mission Santa Ines built in 1804.
Today, it has beautiful gardens that visitors adore.
It's number nineteen of the twenty-one missions.
All were originally built in the Spanish tradition.

N is for Nojoqui Falls, pronounced "NAH-ho-wee."
To find it just follow the trail that is shaded by trees.
It leads you straight back to the 80-foot waterfall.
That sometimes, without rain, will have no water at all.

O is for Ostrich, a giant, flightless bird.
They run in a flock, not in a herd.
A herd is for animals that have four legs, and a flock is for two.
And, yes, there is a difference between an ostrich and an emu!

16

P is for Poppy - our state flower since 1903.
Visitors travel to hike Grass Mountain to see.
After the golden poppy blooms in the spring;
it closes each night and opens in the morning.

Q is for Quail, the California state bird.
They like to stay on the ground but will take flight if disturbed.
If you see one, you're sure to see another—
these plump little birds always stick together.

R is for Rockets that launch way up high.
Best seen in the night when they light up the sky.
With SpaceX, we see Atlas, Delta, and Falcon 9,
Vandenberg's spacecraft is of the best design.

S is for Solvang's windmills, there are at least four.
Go to the Round Tower to begin your tour.
Original Danish windmills are made from wood.
There are metal ones, now, that are just as good.

20

T is for Tarantula, large and peaceful spiders.
They have long legs but they are not fighters.
They crawl out in the heat but home before it's cold.
Female tarantulas can live to be over twenty years old!

21

U is for Up; a reminder to look!
Tilt your head to the sky when you're done with this book.
Hawks, owls or eagles—what can you see?
This land is a wonderful bird sanctuary.

22

V is for Viking, historically known as fierce explorers.
However, they were also businessmen, artists and farmers.
You may recognize them by the horns on their hats,
But did you know they also have their own alphabet?

W is for Walnut trees, once a major local crop.
In the 1950s, farmers planted avocados to swap.
Walnut groves are hidden from our valley to the coast.
There is still an original walnut farm in Los Alamos.

X is for Xus, you want to pronounce it as "hoos".
Easy to remember since it rhymes with loose.
In the native Chumash language, it means "bear".
So, if you happen to see a loose xus, beware!

Y is for Yellow Mustard, a tall vibrant flower.
It's pretty to look at but it has spreading power.
An explorer may have used seeds to mark a spot here.
Now, it covers the coast, so that one spot is not clear.

Z is for Zaca, a word that means "quiet place."
You may see it describe several types of space.
Like a creek, a lake, or even a business.
Zaca is the entire valley of Santa Ynez.

27

About the Author

Author Jenifer Sanregret moved to the Santa Ynez Valley in 2016 with her husband Grant, son Vance, and baby Hayes on the way. She instantly fell in love with the diverse, majestic beauty of the Valley, but had no idea how truly unique it was. Since then, Jenifer has been actively learning, experiencing, and writing about all the amazing little and big things that make up this incredible place she now calls home. When not writing, Jenifer spends her free time with her family hiking, gardening, and exploring all that the S.Y.V. has to offer.

Works Cited

Byrd, Deborah, and Claudia Crowley. "SpaceX's Cool Night Launch And Landing On October 7." *Earth Sky*, 8 Oct. 2018, earthsky. org/todays-image/spacex-falcon9-night-launch-photos-oct-7-2018/.

"California Quail." *State Symbols USA*, statesymbolsusa.org/symbol-official-item/california/state-bird/california-valley-quail.

Chateau Versailles, en.chateauversailles.fr/discover/history/key-dates/first-hot-air-balloon-flight.

"Chumash Animal Words." *Native-Languages*, www.native-languages.org/chumash_animals.htm.

Dozois, Pamela. "Silent Sentinels Have Stood for 50 Years." *Santa Ynez Valley Star*, 15 Feb. 2018, pp. 12–13.

"Fun Facts About Solvang California." *Solvang USA*, 2 Apr. 2019, www.solvangusa.com/media/fun-facts-about-solvang-california/.

"History Summary." *Mission Santa Ines*, missionsantaines.org/history-summary.

Noer, Kurt Evald. "Viking Runes Guide | Runic Alphabet Meanings | Norse / Nordic Letters." *Sons of Vikings*, 28 Feb. 2017, sonsofvikings.com/blogs/history/viking-runes-guide-runic-alphabet-meanings-nordic-celtic-letters.

Norris, Jim. *Los Olivos*. Arcadia Publishing , 2008.

Redmon, Michael. "Santa Barbara Was Once a Walnut Capital of the U.S." *Santa Barbara Independent*, 28 Sept. 2016, www. independent.com/2016/09/28/santa-barbara-was-once-walnut-capital-u-s/.

Sawe, Benjamin Elisha. "What Are The Differences Between An Emu And An Ostrich?" *World Atlas* , 14 Aug. 2019, www. worldatlas.com/articles/what-are-the-differences-between-an-emu-and-an-ostrich.html.

Sherrill, Kathleen. "Ballard School History." *Ballard Schoolhouse History*, Ballard School District, 1996, www.ballardschool.org/ history.aspx.

"Tarantula." *Los Padres Forest Watch*, lpfw.org/our-region/wildlife/tarantula/.

"Vandenberg SFB Launch History." *Space Archive Info*, Vandenberg Air Force Blog, 23 May 2021, www.spacearchive.info/vafblog.htm.

Waaijer , Stefka. "Why Walk on Wooden Shoes." *Holland vs Netherlands*, 21 Nov. 2012, hollandvsnetherlands.wordpress. com/2012/11/21/why-walk-on-wooden-shoes/#:~:text=The%20Dutch%20have%20been%20wearing,and%20 poplar%20woods%20were%20used.

Wilhelm, Menaka, and Greta Mart. "Central Coast Curious: How Did Mustard 'Invade' Our Coast?" *Kcbx.org*, 12 Oct. 2018, www. kcbx.org/post/central-coast-curious-how-did-mustard-invade-our-coast#stream/0.